Etchings of the First Quarter of 2020

Letters, Ideas, Conversations and Poems

Sabarna Roy

ISBN 978-93-90040-55-1
Copyright © Sabarna Roy, 2020

First published in India 2021 by Leadstart Inkstate
A Division of One Point Six Technologies Pvt Ltd

Sales Office:
Unit No.25/26, Building No.A/1,
Near Wadala RTO,
Wadala (East), Mumbai – 400037 India
Phone: +91 969933000
Email: info@leadstartcorp.com
www.leadstartcorp.com

Editor: Sita Bhaskar
Cover: Ami Parekh
Layouts: Victor Patali

For my Japani Bhutia

If there is one thing one can always yearn for and sometimes
attain, it is human love.
- The Plague, Albert Camus

OTHER BOOKS BY SABARNA ROY

Pentacles

Frosted Glass

Abyss

Winter Poems

Random Subterranean Mosaic: 2012 - 2018 Time Frozen in
Myriad Thoughts

About The Author

Sabarna Roy is the author of five books: *Pentacles, Frosted Glass, Abyss, Winter Poems, and Random Subterranean Mosaic: 2012 - 2018 Time Frozen in Myriad Thoughts*. A civil engineer by profession (he passed out from Jadavpur University in 1988), Roy spends his time on books, music, movies and international television series, when he is not writing or at work in an engineering-manufacturing organization in Kolkata. With no love for pets or gardening (although he loves forests and wildlife) or socializing, and a lot of time for introspection and deep (and not-so-deep!) thinking, Roy's works reflect his views on the global order and individuals striving to find their place in it.

Table of Contents

Duality 11

Part-A: A Letter to a Step-daughter 13

Part-B: A Letter to Suranjana 19

Part-C: Nocturnal Conversation between
a Step-father and Step-daughter
over desserts and coffee 27

WINTER POEMS 2020 51

Duality

Part-A: A Letter to a Step-daughter

Part-B: A Letter to Suranjana

Part-C: Nocturnal Conversation between a Step-father and Step-daughter over desserts and coffee

Kolkata
March 20, 2020

Part-A

A Letter to a Step-daughter

Dear Tulip:

You will be glad to know that I now have a technical book, titled: *Articles on Ductile Iron Pipelines and Framework Agreement Methodology,* which covers nine of my technical papers published in peer-reviewed national and international Journals. This book has been published by Scholars' Press, Latvia, European Union.

The book attempts to elaborate the use of Ductile Iron Pipelines in Irrigation application, Gravity Sewer application, Wet Ash Slurry application, Restrained Joint application and use in Steep incline and Hilly terrain, Life Cycle Cost Analysis between various kinds of pipe materials, Feasibility of Recycled Waste Water for Irrigation, a deliberation on Framework Agreement Procurement Methodology and Emerging Challenges in Pipe Distribution Network based Irrigation Projects.

Sorry for boring you with unnecessary facts.

I am also working on my sixth literary project and have been invited to the Kolkata Literary Meet as a panel member to discuss about "Dark Side of the Mind" where I plan to take up issues related to post-modern anxieties. There are many other wonderful sessions with celebrated authors, which I will attend as a delegate. I hope to meet a few interesting people during the day.

There is a festival dinner invitation at the end of the day at Taj Bengal, which I intend to attend briefly. Can we meet at The Park for dessert and coffee?

The other day I happened to glance at your father, who has held on to his athleticism even at this age. Twelve years ago, he was a great athlete and I was a short pot-bellied senior engineering professional and an author. It is a deep mystery to me that your mother abandoned him and chose me all of a sudden. I warn you: I still remain short and pot-bellied and am addicted to my engineering profession and my profession as an author.

Over the years, I have seen you blossoming into a wonderful woman; good looking, kind and a sharp, witty individual. I am your step-father, but at some level I do think, I am your father, because I would like to believe your creative-self would not have bloomed the way it has, had I not been a part of your growing up years. Now that you are grown-up and a creative woman, I seek validation of my art from you.

You know that all my life I have been overpowered by the idea of duality. To make my point explicable, I pen a poem for you to enjoy.

I broke Sandy's arms
I broke Sandy's spinal chord
I broke Sandy's legs
I hammered Sandy's Adam's apple with a spanner
I put a rusted rod through his spleen and lungs
With a stick I fractured his pelvic girdle

He stopped breathing, tired and
Broken and splintered into smithereens

Viscous in a fountain-like pool of blood, sweat, saliva and body juices

My hate fuming like a raging furnace, unceasing molten metal

I thought death will square my anger; it did not

I wanted Sandy to get up and resist me deliriously
So that I could punch, paw, bite and tear flesh from his bones
Mix his blood with gasoline and throw at him back with a burning matchstick

He would burn
But not turn to ashes

Burn forever

To resonate my hate

What Sandy could do, I never could

Sandy laughed freely while I got depressed with each passing day
The plasma within oscillating in frenzy in unknown agony

Sandy explored the marine world – star fishes, octopuses, jelly fishes, eels, sea-horses, corals and gold fishes – while I wanted to stick to my dungeon

Sandy made love while I wanted to violate women

Sandy wanted to reform: he always spoke of integrity and ethics

I loved cutting deals, by hook or crook; I looked at anybody as competition and abhorred it

Yet, we returned to each other in one body

Sandy, an angel and I, an untamed beast

I know you are at the cusp of venturing into marine conservation. We will discuss duality, my ideas around duality and marine conservation, when we meet for our desserts and coffee session at The Park on January 22.

Love,

Babazula

Part-B
A Letter to Suranjana

Dear Suranjana:

I must first congratulate you for conducting a wonderful session yesterday: Dark Side of the Mind at KLM. I enjoyed it to the hilt.

I thought I would explain my position on **Lolita** so that I am not misunderstood and also because you were my sister's senior at BGKV.

The first point I wanted to make was: There is a scientific distinction between pedophiles/infantophiles and child molesters/violators of women out in the open. This was my limited point.

Now, let us turn our focus on **Lolita**.

Let us look at the story of **Lolita** from a certain point in time with my commentary in […]:

… Disbelieving Humbert's false assurance that the diary is a sketch for a future novel, Charlotte runs out of the house to send the letters but is killed by a swerving car. Humbert destroys the letters and retrieves Dolores from camp, claiming that her mother has fallen seriously ill and has been hospitalised. He then takes her to a high-end hotel that Charlotte had earlier recommended. Humbert knows he will feel guilty **[which means, Humbert is capable of feeling guilt; he is not unconscionable]** if he consciously rapes Dolores, and so tricks her into taking sedatives in her ice cream. As he waits for the pill to take effect, he wanders through the hotel and meets a mysterious man who seems to be aware of Humbert's plan for Dolores. Humbert excuses himself from the conversation and returns to the hotel room. There, he discovers that he had been fobbed with a milder drug, as Dolores is merely drowsy and wakes up frequently, drifting in and out of sleep. He dares not touch her that night. In the morning, Dolores reveals to Humbert that she actually has already lost her virginity, having engaged in sexual activity with an older boy at a different camp a year ago **[is it true or a lie (?); if it is true it seems it was consensual; if it is a lie we have to accept Lolita is capable of grave lies]**. After leaving the hotel, Humbert reveals to Dolores that her mother is dead.

Humbert and Dolores travel across the country, driving all day and staying in motels. Humbert desperately tries to maintain Dolores's interest in travel and himself, and increasingly bribes her in exchange for sexual favours **[this is gravely criminal in content and intent]**. They finally settle in Beardsley, a small New England town. Humbert adopts the role of Dolores's father and enrolls her in a local private school for girls. Humbert jealously and strictly controls all of Dolores's social gatherings and forbids her from dating and attending parties. It is only at the instigation of the school headmaster, who regards Humbert as a strict and conservative European parent, that he agrees to Dolores's participation in the school play, the title of which is the same as the hotel in which Humbert met the mysterious man. The day before the premiere of the performance, a serious quarrel breaks out between Dolores and Humbert, and Dolores runs out of the house. When Humbert finds her a few moments later, she tells him that she wants to leave town and continue traveling **[Lolita exerts her own will for the first time]**. Humbert is initially delighted, but as he travels, he becomes increasingly suspicious – he feels that he is being followed by someone Dolores is familiar with. The man following them is Clare Quilty – a friend of Charlotte and a famous playwright who wrote the play that Dolores was to participate in. In the Colorado Mountains, Dolores falls ill. Humbert checks her into a local hospital, from where she is discharged one night by her "uncle". Humbert knows she has no living relatives and he immediately embarks on a frantic search to find Dolores and her abductor, but ultimately fails. For the next two years, Humbert barely sustains himself in a moderately functional relationship with a young alcoholic named Rita. Deeply depressed **[we know Humbert is diseased because of his unbridled lust for Lolita],** Humbert unexpectedly receives a letter from Dolores, now 17, telling him that she is married, pregnant, and in desperate need of money **[can we say Lolita is manipulating Humbert (?)]**. Humbert, armed with a pistol, tracks down Dolores's address and gives her the money, which was due as an inheritance from her mother **[in financial matters Humbert is revealed to be equitable]**. Humbert learns that Dolores's husband, a deaf mechanic, is not her abductor. Dolores reveals to Humbert that Quilty took her from the hospital and that she was in love with him, but she was rejected when she refused to star in one of his pornographic films **[Lolita knows where to draw a line and make an independent choice].** Dolores also rejects Humbert's request to leave with him [Lolita knows where to draw a line and make an independent choice]. Humbert goes to the drug-addled Quilty's mansion and shoots him several times **[is it some kind of a revenge of love (?)]**. Shortly afterward, Humbert is arrested, and in his closing thoughts, he reaffirms his love for Dolores **[he risks himself by such affirmation]** and asks for his memoir to be withheld from public release until after her death. Dolores dies in childbirth on Christmas Eve, 1952.

Your view about Lolita is the majority view among critics.

There is a minority view as well. A minority of critics have accepted Humbert's version of events at face value. In 1958, Dorothy Parker described the novel as "the engrossing, anguished story of a man, a man of taste and culture, who can love only little girls" and Lolita as "a dreadful little creature, selfish, hard, vulgar, and foul-tempered". In 1959, novelist Robertson Davies excused the narrator entirely, writing that the theme of Lolita is "not the corruption of

an innocent child by a cunning adult, but the exploitation of a weak adult by a corrupt child. This is no pretty theme, but it is one with which social workers, magistrates and psychiatrists are familiar."

<u>My view is neither the majority view nor the minority view. I look at Humbert and Lolita in light of historical and contextual reference. Humbert's lust for Lolita is unsettling and causes everlasting damage to the way he craves for Lolita. His crime is: He does not allow Lolita to grow up independently and uses his financial and age-related might on her. But, I will not go to the extent of calling him a violator or a rapist. It is corrupted love that is primal to his actions. YES, I WOULD NOT FEEL COMFORTABLE IF HUMBERT IS NEAR MY DAUGHTER. AT THE SAME TIME I WOULD NOT LIKE MY DAUGHTER TO BE LOLITA – a skewed product of American initial consumerism and pop-culture.</u>

Like all classics, Lolita presents before us a very amorphous reality that shows us extremes in which human life exists.

With affectionate regards,

Sabarna Da

Part-C

Nocturnal Conversation between a Step-father and Step-daughter over desserts and coffee

In life, there are certain things that are within our control, and a lot many things that are beyond our control. The aggregate of determinate and indeterminate factors makes life indeterminate. Uncertainty is closely associated with indeterminateness as indeterminate problems are likely to have multiple solutions.

[Babazula has been vociferous about Anna Karenina by Leo Tolstoy for a long time]

Anna Karenina was a doting wife and mother who abandoned her family and home in pursuit of passionate love for another man. The union with her lover did not satisfy her soul. She remained restless, and desirous of more and more love, and in painful agony for her son whom she left. Her insurmountable love for her lover did not stop her from casting an influence or charm on other men. Her anxieties led her to inflicting death upon herself. At no point in time through the entire voluminous novel are we in a position to predict what Anna will do next. It is as if there are multiple Annas that are driving her in self-contradictory directions.

When Anna Karenina was written, the influence of genes on man's actions was not well understood. The authors of that time and until much later would meticulously detail the physical circumstances around a character so that the readers could understand why somebody behaved the way they did. Yet, the readers in the greatest of texts found something amiss. With greater understanding of genetics, authors understood that along with immediate physical context, family behaviour and lineage are of great significance. Their texts soon got modified.

[Babazula has been vociferous about Nikhilesh's economic views in Ghare Baire by Rabi Thakur for a very long time]

In Ghare Baire, Nikhilesh walks two self-contradictory paths. He sincerely wants his wife to embrace Western thought and education. On economy, he prefers imported goods to goods manufactured in India, though on cost-effective grounds, domestic goods would be financially viable for peasants working on his farms and estates. In the first instance, he exhibits the demeanour of a benevolent elite exposed to English education and ways. Whereas, in the second instance, he is clearly opposed to national entrepreneurs, exposing his feudal roots. Nikhilesh does not evolve to become a national entrepreneur on the strength of financial surplus [capital] amassed through farm-produce-tax, but in the world of ideas makes a quantum jump to internationalism only on the strength of his education, which can at best be fragile.

[Babazula's moot point about Duality is]

Classical physics and how we would think in the years to come would change forever when light was first considered to be wave-particle; gravity a field and not force. Also when the quantum of uncertainty in defining a particle's location and/or momentum for the collision between the observatory field and the particle's own field was mathematically established. This impacted social theory, literature and arts, and artistic and aesthetics theory.

Fundamental to everything was the recognition of duality, which many years back was postulated by Hegel in his master-slave theory. We could be slaves, masters, slave-masters, and master-slaves in varying orders. This is better understood with the post-modern development of psychiatry.

[Babazula attended a session on Schizophrenia at the Literary Meet and got a copy of the presentation made there and read out to Tulip]

Oliver John Mason of Research Department of Clinical, Educational and Health Psychology, University College London, London, UK concludes in his Opinion Article dated September 14, 2014, titled: "The duality of schizotypy: is it both dimensional and categorical?", as follows:

"Overall, I have attempted to argue that even in the non-pathological domain of schizotypal individual differences there are numerous possibilities for both dimensional and categorical expressions both of traits and states. Taxonomic [which means, concerned with the classification of things] expression has greater support for negative schizotypal features such as anhedonia [which means, the inability to feel pleasure] and potentially some associated neurocognitive features; positive schizotypy, on the other hand, sees much empirical support for "true" dimensionality at both genotype [which means, the genetic constitution of an individual organism] and phenotypic [which means, relating to the observable characteristics of an individual resulting from the interaction of its genotype with the environment] expression. Even here, however, there is room for gene–environment interactions and epigenetics [which means, the study of changes in organisms caused by modification of gene expression rather than alteration of the genetic code itself] to produce discontinuous results."

"As a rider to this final point, it is apposite [which means, apt in the circumstances] to point out that there may equally be important phenotypic consequences for schizotypy in the absence of a pathogenic environment or the presence of a protective factor such as high cognitive or emotional intelligence. Thus, positive schizotypy is also associated with a range of "healthy" or at least adaptive outcomes. Again, paralleling the advantages seen with cluster analytic approaches, Tabak and Weisman de Mamani identified several schizotypal latent profiles: the negative/disorganised schizotypy profile had the poorest levels of well-being and schizotypes [which means, one who suffers from a mental disorder characterised by severe social anxiety, thought disorder, paranoid ideation, derealization, transient psychosis and often unconventional beliefs] solely with positive features had the highest – commensurate with non-schizotypes. Taking a similar latent profile analytic approach to a non-clinical sample, Hori et al described 15% as "high-positive-schizotypy/ adaptive" and possessing of high self-directedness, cooperativeness, and self-transcendence. This is consistent with growing evidence of the highly creative and spiritual outcomes for some schizotypal individuals, and may point to the operation of antagonistic pleiotropy [which means, occurs when one gene influences two or more seemingly unrelated phenotypic traits] or genetic linkage such that schizotypal traits survived throughout our evolutionary history."

<u>Myth: Schizophrenia means you have a split personality.</u>

Reality: This is a classic myth. A split personality, also called a Dissociative Identity Disorder or a Multiple Personality Disorder, is extraordinarily rare, and debatable. It is quite distinct from schizophrenia. Schizophrenia is a thought disorder. The myth likely stems from the fact that in schizophrenia there is a breakdown, or split, between thoughts, emotions, and behaviour.

This split results in a disconnect between reality and fantasy. The person may experience delusions and hallucinations, and emotions may become blunted or inappropriate. When most people think of schizophrenia, they think of someone who is seeing things and hearing voices. These are what are called positive symptoms, but people with schizophrenia have negative symptoms, too. Among the common negative symptoms are low motivation, difficulty forming social connections, and a flat, blunted effect. A lack of pleasure in everyday activities, rarely speaking, and difficulty paying attention are also symptoms, according to the American Psychological Association.

[Babuzula was confronted by a Marxist at the Literary Meet where Babazula made his points on Marxian thought referring to Chapter 63 of his RANDOM SUBTERRANEAN MOSAIC: 2012 - 2018]

Karl Marx's two greatest contributions in political economy are as follows:

1. Alienation theory postulated in The Economic and Philosophic Manuscripts of 1844.

2. Surplus theory (M – C – M – C ...) postulated in Das Kapital (1867).

He concluded that capitalism would crumble because of its inherent conflicts and lead to a revolution by the proletariat, taking over means of production by who produce (participate by giving their labour) and not the class that invests capital in enterprises, which would lead to inequities being reversed.

However, Marx failed to establish:

1. The road-map of such a revolution leading to the capture of economic power – the nature of the entity that would represent the common interests of the proletariat. Later Lenin theorised that it would be the Communist Party.

2. The concrete nature and dynamics of a post-revolution society.

3. How industrial society would proceed towards

destruction of the ecology comprehensively.

4. Reduction of a human being's identity to political economics, which gravely negated all other pluralities.

5. How history as a history of class struggles was only assumed to be a fact in the Communist Manifesto. History was not studied empirically to demonstrate this alleged fact.

6. Whether the proletariat would retain its revolutionary capacity as the means of production and living conditions bettered pursuant to economic movements, militant or otherwise.

7. The relationship between the development of human brain and prolonged malnourishment due to years and years and years of impoverishment. The proletariat of the capitalist society were mostly the progeny of landless peasants of a feudal society. Could thought leaders have emerged out of this class, having undergone the duress of relentless economic inequity, because of which their brains could not have been fully developed due to abject poverty and hunger?

We also have to appreciate that Karl Marx existed in a time which was defined by Newtonian Physics and Euclidian Geometry and his study was mostly limited to the British, French, German and later, the North American economies. 20th century brought mass-production, quantum physics, tensor calculus, computers, artificial intelligence, advanced genetic engineering, advanced anthropological studies, which collectively turned upside down many, many assumptions and wisdom of the earlier centuries. Socio-politically speaking, 20th century brought forward practice of democracies (a system of forcing political equality upon economic inequality, and this forced political equality fails to alleviate the inbuilt economic inequality), imperialism, neo-colonialism, consumerism, hyper-consumerism, identity-wars, terrorism, climate change, advent of neo-capitalism, disproportionate growth of economy among nation-states following different economic models.

Plekhanov brought Marxism to Czarist Russia (which was primarily feudal and laced with inhuman oppression), and Lenin revolutionised it theoretically and practically, resulting in the Bolshevik Revolution of 1917. It failed gradually over the years. I summarise the following reasons principally based on my study of the Bolshevik experiment:

1. It is not the proletariat who captured power of the state, it was the Communist Party: assumed to approximate the proletariat; a party that comprised valourous intellectual elite, political, and military strategists. The political power was ferociously centralised. Capitalists were replaced by political bureaucrats and technocrats.

2. Industry was given the primary focus to economic growth, thereby, competing with the Western world instead of finding a unique way to exist more harmoniously, ecologically and in a decentralised manner.

3. The citadels of arts, culture, and free-independent thinking were overturned, crushing everything that keeps a civilization alive.

Incompleteness of the Marxist thought or the failure of the Bolshevik experiment do not prove Marx wrong. To my mind, Marxian thought is a scientific socio-economic-political theory rooted in political economy of its time and based on revolutionary imagination and intuition. Like Einstein's General Theory of Relativity. Einstein's intuitions are being proven till this day, which means the scientific framework postulated by Einstein is getting further expanded and validated with time.

What happened with Marx was, because of his theory's altruistic aims, revolutionaries wanted to adapt his theory to validate their ideas of a social and political revolution. His theory should have been given time to integrate with emerging realities. It should have been made into a more forceful, ever-emerging and visionary economic and political idea. People like Trotsky tried but faced death at the hands of Stalin. There have been many other Trotskys and many other Stalins in history. Sadly.

[Tulip made her points on Marine Conservation to Babazula]

Earth's biological diversity is being destroyed very rapidly. In the next half-century—less than one human lifetime—the Earth could lose blue whales, giant pandas, tigers, black rhinoceroses and millions of lesser-known species. Entire ecosystems, such as tropical dry forests, mangroves, and floodplain rivers could be damaged beyond repair. Our planet is now facing the most devastating biological catastrophe in the last 65 million years, since a huge asteroid hit the Earth and caused appalling damage, killing off the dinosaurs and more than half of the planet's other species. But today's mass extinction has a very different cause: the way we humans live our lives.

Since the early 1980's, increasing attention has been paid to the importance of biodiversity and to the number of species being depleted at an alarming rate. Many biologists believe that we are in the midst of a mass extinction because the rate of species loss is higher now than ever before. It is estimated that between 17,000 and 100,000 species are eliminated each year. Studies have shown that as many as one in eight plant species are threatened with extinction. The majority of these losses are due to human activity, particularly habitat destruction as more and more land gets usurped for human use.

The hot issue of global destruction of rainforests, coral reefs, mangroves, and other rich habitats is being addressed by conservation organisations and by global legislation to try and reverse damaging trends and encourage sustainable management of resources.

Some of the basic threats to biodiversity include:

- Increasing human populations out of balance with the scale of natural resources

- Heavy consumption and excessive exploitation of natural resources

- Lack of sufficient knowledge and understanding of species and ecosystems

- Destruction of ecosystems and habitats due to increased land use, urbanization, and pollution

- Underestimating the value of nature and its resources

- Global climate change

- Ecological disasters such as large-scale fires and floods

New global agreements, such as the Convention on Biological Diversity mentioned above, are helping nations recognise the existing value of their natural resources and its value to future generations. The Convention was developed during the 1992 Earth Summit in Rio de Janeiro where world leaders agreed on a comprehensive strategy for "sustainable development" that meets our needs while ensuring that the Earth's resources will be sustained for future generations. This agreement established good stewardship of these resources as nations continue to build economic development. The three main goals of the Convention are:

- Conservation of biological diversity

- Sustainable use of its components

- Fair and equitable sharing of the benefits from the use of genetic resources

The agreement commits countries to conserving biodiversity, developing tools for sustainability, and sharing the benefits.

[Babazula made a few Intervening Thoughts]

From computers to Internet to Robotics to Artificial/ Applied Intelligence to Machine Learning and very penetrative understanding of genes and gene modification and anthropology we have traversed to an era of Internet of Things and Services. Smart Technology can provide enormous free time to people in an intensely inequitable and polarised world with climate change threatening to erode the planet within a few years.

With vast learning at man's disposal the burning question is: How would it use its resources to revert the process of extinction of human civilization?

[Babazula made the opening remarks about Love]

In spite of mammoth inventions, and discoveries of mankind, we have not been able to fully grasp the duality of love, and lust in human relationships.

In The Museum of Innocence, Pamuk establishes a tale of pure love between Kemal Bey and Fuzun [his cousin]. In The Unbearable Lightness of Being, Kundera establishes a lustful yarn between Tomas and Sabina. All of us are swinging between the extremes of this pendulum. Where and how we exist at any given point in time is very complex to figure out.

[Tulip discussed the hidden love story of TS Eliot]

Let us look at a real life example of unrequited love!

A collection of more than 1,000 letters from the Nobel Laureate TS Eliot to his confidante and muse Emily Hale was unveiled in the first week of 2020, after having been kept in sealed boxes at a US university library for 60 years.

The cache promises to offer an intimate insight into the poet's life and work, and on his relationship with Hale, a source of speculation for decades.

The 1,131 letters, which date from between 1930 and 1956, were donated by Hale to Princeton University Library more than 60 years ago with her stipulation they remain sealed until 50 years after either Eliot's death, or her own, whichever occurred last. He died in 1965, and she in 1969.

The two had met in Cambridge, Massachusetts, in 1912, when Eliot attended Harvard. They rekindled their friendship in 1927, by which time Eliot had moved to England. He corresponded frequently with Hale, who was from Boston, and who taught drama at US universities including Scripps College in California.

Eliot ordered Hale's letters to him to be burned, according to biographers.

"I think it's perhaps the literary event of the decade," Anthony Cuda, an Eliot scholar and director of the TS

Eliot International Summer School, told the Associated Press. "I don't know of anything more awaited or significant. It's momentous to have these letters coming out."

Their relationship "must have been incredibly important and their correspondence must have been remarkably intimate for him to be so concerned about the publication," he added.

Eliot was born in St Louis, Missouri, in 1888. His best known works include The Waste Land, The Hollow Men and Four Quartets.

His letters to Hale began after the end of his first marriage to the Cambridge governess Vivienne Haigh-Wood. Scholars point to the first poem in the Quartets series, called Burnt Norton, as significant because of lines that suggest missed opportunities and what might have been. Burnt Norton was named after a home in England Eliot visited with Hale. Eliot married his second wife, Valerie Fletcher, in 1957.

The Eliot scholar Frances Dickey, one of the editors of The Complete Prose of TS Eliot, said the poet was ashamed of his first marriage. The letters could reveal how close he and Hale were, and if they ever considered marriage, she said. Whatever else Hale was, she said, she was a link to the life he had left behind in the US.

The 12 boxes, which include photographs, ephemera and clippings, were unsealed by Princeton University Library staff in October 2019 to be scanned for digital viewing at the library from 2 January.

Susan Stewart, a professor of English at Princeton, who was present at the unsealing, said two senior librarians "stood behind a table full of wooden crates wielding dual pairs of tin snips."

"They proceeded in tandem to snap the copper bands holding the crates and the wooden slats clattered to the table."

She added that what little was known about the correspondence indicated "Eliot wrote to Hale freely about his predilections, his fellow poets, and above all, his opinions as a reader".

Daniel Linke, the interim head of special collections at the library, said there was minimal, if any reading, during the unsealing. He expected that scholars from around the world would be travelling to Princeton in the first few days.

"It will be the special collections equivalent of a stampede at a rock concert," he told the Associated Press.

[Babazula gives a few examples on Dualities]

Another duality is the transition of a tyrant to a benevolent, or a benevolent to a tyrant. Such revolutionary transitions happen because of traumatic circumstances. Real life stands testimony to this phenomenon.

Another duality is peace of solitude and craving for an audience.

The other two often faced dualities are:

1. How will we achieve true empathy? By intellectual understanding and realization or practice. It can be argued that it is a fine balance of both.

2. In making an invention how much of it is an intricate combination of imagination and intuition, or rigorous experimentation, collection and interpretation of results. Similarly, here it can be argued that it is a fine balance of both.

[Babazula and Tulip agree to conclude]

Can we conclude that: Everything is in a state of constant transition and it is change which is constant?

In an era of uncontrolled greed and hunger for power, how will mankind realise its infinitesimally small place in the universe? In this river of life, how will mankind achieve transitional duality and not constancy?

WINTER POEMS 2020

WINTER POEMS 2020

The sweet rush of death

Through the winter rains
From the pacing waters of Ganga flowing along Banaras
city
From the burning pyres on one embankment
From the small dunes of sand on the other
From the rotting steel of an ancient bridge

The scent of shameless youth and life are gone
The sweet rush of death, all over

Do not listen to me: For I have no hope to give
Mainak, who is dying by the hour
Is strapped to his bed with tumours in his stomach
Refusing medication and hospitalisation
A no to live by artificial means
He holds my hands with his frail long fingers
An artist of epic murals – crisscrossing the globe, a few
years back
Metropolitan railway stations, bulbous airports and
heritage sites
Locking my hands to his, urging me to tell him
Sinuous stories of cops and goons
He listens attentively and then dozes off to pale sleep,
lightly snoring

Outside, on the streets
The cymbals and drums are playing
The students might uproot this deathly government

The sweet rush of death, all over in my mind

In the evenings, I walk to the Cantonment area
Woods, grasslands, bougainvillea, ponds and golf carts
Some rest, coffee, sandwiches and then, back to
Mainak

The sweet rush of death lingers in my mind
In a few days, Mainak will be gone

Memories, murals and unfinished artwork are all that
will be left
Of this ferociously handsome man, once upon a time

The sweet rush of death
The sounds of cymbals and drums
The roaring sounds of youth all over

Kolkata
January 11, 2020

Leaves of fig and leaves of maple floating in air like
tarot cards
Rustle of an unknown breeze flowing through the
leaves, a strange music
Herds of deer running in slow motion
Aroma of tender life radiating
Green snakes and shining foxes are waking up
Aboriginal couples rising up from their shaking slumber
– they had a feast of food and love

The scent is everywhere

The fire is coming

The fire is coming

Ashes, ashes and ashes everywhere

Kolkata
January 12, 2020

The scent of my city changes during the winters

Children – with tennis-ball-like-cheeks – from schools
go on picnics with their boisterous teachers in colourful
dresses with homemade delicacies trapped inside
Chinese tiffin boxes – aroma of egg and chicken rolls
Fragrance of perfumes and talcum powder floating
from their teachers' bodies
Lovers   meet   around   curated   water-bodies   and
exchange colourful, blooming flowers
The old go for longer morning walks oblivious of their
throbbing knee pain; ending the sojourn with a cup of
steaming syrupy milk tea, shingaras and jalebis

The rich have parties at clubs, banquets, lawns and 5
star resorts
They have very different ambience, scents and noises
– inaccessible and mysterious
The shine on their cars is another thing to watch

My city is also teeming with
Hopeless,   unemployed,   starving   and   mentally
challenged people
Their faces and destinies crisscrossed with scars

They shiver in the winters till they freeze
They have very little access to shelter – blankets and
quilts, water, and food

They decay in their relentless thirst and hunger – the
stench goes up to the sky

I do not know what to do in the winters
Whether to join the children, the lovers, the old, the
rich or the disenfranchised

I go my way – through the suburban shrubs and sit
the whole day along a secret pond with my fishing net,
sunshine warming my shoulders and back, waiting for
my frugal catch – and, in the evening go to Baba's
house to oil-fry my catch for Baba so that he can devour
them gradually with his single peg of Jack Daniels

I read out Osip Mandelstam to him – some lines he can
hear; some lines he cannot

When I bid him farewell, he grips me in his embrace
and croons in my ears –
This winter will pass

Kolkata
January 13, 2020

In the unending fields of mustard – sprawling vineyards
On a narrow embankment of mushy soil
I dig up a trench with a spade and a pickaxe
Very deep
Very dark

It takes a full day to prepare the trench with a bed of
leaves – moist and dried
Collected in the adjacent jungles in the preceding days
tirelessly

There are some bread loaves and marmalade

The quilt with embroidered print of deer and peacocks
playing in the woods
Was stitched by my paternal grandmother

Night oozes out of the sky
Darkness struggling with the yellow haze emanating
out of
The fields of mustard brought to life, as if by a celestial
magic wand

I enter my trench
Eat some loaves with marmalade
Pull the quilt over my body
And, look up at the sky

I feel intoxicated by the sighting of stars, planets and

moons – galaxies and constellations
It reminds me of my days of working as a spy
For states with multiple faces and faceless states

The cemeteries of Tokyo in skyscrapers
The brothels of Zurich
My lazy journeys from London to Cotswold
My lazy journeys from Paris to Giverny
The serrated rooftops of Istanbul
The breakfast shops in Lower Manhattan

Then the darkness of Congo, Sudan and the forests of
Bastar in India

A strange light in my trench – a concoction of the
night's darkness
And, the light glowing and melting out of the
innumerable flowers of mustard

I look up at the sky

Tokyo is falling
Zurich is falling
London is falling
Paris is falling
Istanbul is falling

New York is falling

Strange fires spreading across Congo, Sudan and India

I inject a shot in my veins and look at dilapidated cities
– their ruins
Playing in the magical light of the fields of mustard

Fires playing in the distance on the cinemascope of the
night sky

Kolkata
January 14, 2020

I broke Sandy's arms
I broke Sandy's spinal chord
I broke Sandy's legs
I hammered Sandy's Adam's apple with a spanner
I put a rusted rod through his spleen and lungs
With a stick I fractured his pelvic girdle

He stopped breathing, tired and
Broken and splintered into smithereens
Viscous in a pool of blood, sweat, saliva and body
juices

My hate fuming like a raging furnace, unceasing molten
metal

I thought death will square my anger; it did not

I wanted Sandy to get up and resist me deliriously
So that I could punch, paw, bite and tear flesh from
his bones
Mix his blood with gasoline and throw back at him with
a burning matchstick

He would burn
But not turn to ashes

Burn forever

To resonate my hate

What Sandy could do, I never could

Sandy laughed freely while I got depressed with each
passing day
The plasma within oscillating in frenzy in unknown
agony

Sandy explored the marine world – star fishes,
octopuses, jelly fishes, eels, sea-horses, corals and
gold fishes – while I wanted to stick to my dungeon

Sandy made love while I wanted to violate women

Sandy wanted to reform: he always spoke of integrity
and ethics

I loved cutting deals, by hook or crook; I looked at
anybody as competition and abhorred it

Yet, we returned to each other in one body

Sandy, an angel and I, an untamed beast

Kolkata
January 15, 2020

The escalating projectile of savage lust defined Santanu
Every night, he needed a new woman in his bed
He loved conquest
It turned him crazy

Santanu cheated his wife,
His children
His parents
His friends and colleagues

Santanu cheated his lovers
His elite concubines, when he was in short supply of
lovers

Santanu was so turned-on by relentless coquettish
conquests and lying and experimenting with new
women

That he lost sight of where he was going

One spring morning, in 2016, Santanu got up in his
Parisian villa overlooking a thrush of shivering hazel
leaves
He felt a splintering ache in his stomach, an infinite
emptiness in his chest
His vision blurred
He felt like puking

Most of all, he felt monstrously sleepy and as if, he
should run away from this civilization
Somewhere
Where he could rest, shower and rest and shower
And, later have some coffee
Alone

Santanu, felt, ravaged and crumbled and dreamt of a
black hood of death sweeping him over
Was he drawn inside a vortex of shadows of the
treacheries he committed in his life: he pondered

Day-by-day, night-after-night, prickling arrows of guilt
punctured his soul

He wanted to return to his wife
His children
His parents
His friends and colleagues

Who by this time had charted separate pathways

He visited a reputed neuro-psychiatrist, Dr Brahma,
who after listening to the story of his life said in a deep
baritone:

Santanu, love is not an opportunity
It is my dear, grace
You have to be capable of loving and be loved

Consider this emptiness the starting point of your New
Life, healing

Kolkata
January 16, 2020

The banks have beautifully cut grasses
I lie down on the grass carpet
And, look up at the blue azure sky
Some white tufts of clouds here and there
Razor sharp sunshine cuts across chilly air
The muddy river – billowy – flows by
Ships hoot and smokestacks puff grey smoke telling us
tales of distant lands
Boats ferry bank-to-bank with grim passengers,
bicycles and goats

On the embankment road
Guys are selling lottery tickets, chewing gums, ice-
balls, candies
There are balloon sellers
Puffed-rice sellers with mustard oil and spices
Some of them also show you pictures on condom
packets
And, whisper destinations of slut-salons not far from
the river

For a moment, it seems, the planet has come to a stop
It is neither revolving around the sun
Or, rotating around its axis
A thick veil of soundlessness has spread from the
zenith to nadir
It's a freeze-frame

And, then all of a sudden, from the corner of my eye

I glance upon an abandoned horse
With black silken skin
Lost amidst the landscape looking at the river vacuously

A gigantic cargo ship from a Mediterranean land, bells
and bells uproariously
Puffing a long trail of black smoke
Scaring the black horse

I smoke my cigar as furiously as I can
Drink my spiked Grey Goose from a two-pint bottle

Feeling sleepy and endlessly lazy
Remembering Kahlil Gibran's line:
One day you will ask me which is more important. My
life or yours? I will say mine and you will walk away not
knowing that you are my life.
I said this to Monisha in my years of youth almost
ending my life
Almost, ending my life

Kolkata
January 17, 2020

<u>Jallianwala Bagh – 100 years</u>

A full moon night beaming silver
Through a cool veil of tremulous breeze
Caressing the memorial stone, and through the cage
over a dark well, and the bullet spotted masonry walls
Air reflecting, illumination reflecting, through the
condensed memories of
Sounds of gunshots, wails of children and women, and
hissing of human stampede
Screeching orders of a psychopath – soulless –
enervated by the sights of oozing blood, tearing of
flesh, and breaking of bones of unarmed men, and
women, and children
Gathered around to celebrate Baisakhi, and peacefully
protest the arrest, and deportation of
Satyapal, and *Saifuddin Kitchlew*

Dyer entered the garden with his riflemen through the
narrow corridor gate
Unfurling like treacherous waves
Shooting at the entrances
Whoever ran to exit was hit with bullets – either death
or morbid injury, thus fate

The *House of Lords* lauded the action, as *Lords* are
irreverential of the destinies of humans
The *House of Commons* was critical, and censured
Dyer through an investigative committee

Funnily, *Rudyard Kipling* declared at the time: *Dyer* did

his duty as he saw it

Rabi Thakur renounced his knighthood, and fumed:
*such mass murderers aren't worthy of giving any title
to anyone*

The bullet marks preserved on the walls with metallic
jacketed borders
The swarthiness, and the rising dampness up the well
as you look down deeper: as if, screams ricocheting up
the cylinder like a helical matrix, deafening your ears
The rush of crowds running amok to save their lives –
clouds of dust everywhere – chillingly painted on the
art pieces in the memorial museum

Make you think: how one human unleashes such
unbridled cruelty on another human

Are these holocausts of human social design alone
or are there genes embedded, and evolved in our
consciousness that guide us to such
Self-extinction massacres
For holocausts have repeated one after the other –
including on the flora, and fauna that support our life

With all the intelligence that the human race has
We have learnt very little from our life experiences
Sadly

**Kolkata
January 18, 2020**

The sunshine reaches the solitary bungalow roof
Lost within the upper stretches of Rishikesh jungles
Like mist; the canopy of treetops is so thick here
The floors are carpeted with Kashmiri *galichas*
The roofs have ornate Arabic chandeliers
On the wooden walls hang ancient masks of multifarious
cultures and traditions

Dr X called me for a summary interview about why
I attempted self-death a week back
At Haridwar, having jumped into the freezing cold river
when I didn't know how to swim

I told Dr X coldly: It was not a momentary lapse of
reason
The act was premeditated
I felt no joy in life for I have tasted success in every
field I wanted
Except intense love of a beautiful woman

Dr X offered me some sweet *Pahari chai* and spicy
sandwiches and then,
Offered me some advice in his sonorous tone:
Success is not significant; your love in pursuing your
passion is paramount irrespective of consequences
The same with the love of a woman
She will come and stick to you if she is to happen
If she doesn't happen the natural way, you can ask
your Ma to find a woman for you
Maybe with time you will tolerate and love each other

The problem with you is, you are unable to handle
your aloneness

Then his voice rose and he sounded a bit agitated and
thunderous:
There is no harm in asking your Ma for help instead of
torturing her with the loss of her beloved son
And, please learn to swim soon

I am banished after this talk and tea and snack

As I walk down the wooded undulating rocky path, I
feel secure at the thought that Ma would be waiting for
me at home with a bowl of *kumbh matar* that I love to
eat with butter *naan*

I am actually in two minds: should I or should I not ask
her to find a beautiful woman for me from her circle;
would she feel jealous; she has fiercely guarded me
all her life

A few weeks back, I felt doubly jilted by a woman's
betrayal and felt so vanquished for days and nights

I began running, then, almost mad to watch the soft
mysterious glow on Ma's face whenever I reached
home early

Diamond Harbor
January 19, 2020

Crows, mynas, sparrows and pigeons
Gather in my garden
Short cut grasses, hibiscus, clivia, orchids and jasmine
Colours and fragrance lingering in the air

The birds play around and look for their food within
the grass mat
Butterflies – atrophaneura semperi – fly from flower
to flower

I sit in my armchair with a vintage copy of The Plague
This book and its accompanying literature I have read
and reread many, many times over
For I have to teach my students at the University and
earn my daily living

After all these years I am still awestruck by this book

Some of the underlined passages I reread to the birds,
butterflies, grass mat and flowers in my garden:

*Tarrou nodded. 'Yes. But your victories will never be
lasting; that's all.' Rieux's face darkened. 'Yes, I know
that. But it's no reason for giving up the struggle.'*

*No, Father. I've a very different idea of love. And until
my dying day, I shall refuse to love a scheme of things
in which children are put to torture.*

*What's natural is the microbe. All the rest — health,
integrity, purity (if you like) — is a product of the*

human will, of a vigilance that must never falter. The good man, the man who infects hardly anyone, is the man who has the fewest lapses of attention.

I have been fascinated by the character of Dr Rieux, who to my mind is the idealised Rebel

About his love Camus writes, during Rieux's struggle inside the city afflicted with the epidemic:

All this time he'd practically forgotten the woman he loved, so absorbed had he been in trying to find a rift in the walls that cut him off from her. But at this same moment, now that once more all ways of escape were sealed against him, he felt his longing for her blaze up again.

A sparrow and a butterfly sit on my copy of The Plague and they do not allow me to read anymore

Two mynas sit on each shoulder

I look up at the sky; the blue melts from it like molten metal

I can feel the time has come to leave my home and run into the jungles where a drama is being played out in the amphitheater of the life of our nation

Kolkata
January 20, 2020

Dr X has a zoo in his suburban villa
The trophies in his collection are a South African
leopard and a rattle snake from Central Argentina

Dr X narrated stories about how he got his trophies
that he nurtured laboriously personally –
Nourishment, warmth, washing and cleaning their
shelter and daily routines and chores to be followed

I am afraid of these terrible looking animals
Dr X tells me, they are handsome to the point of
arousing ones libido
I do not argue; I keep quiet

Dr X asks me, how it would feel to be temporarily
chased by his prized catches
A cold sensation runs down my spine
I keep quiet again

One early, cold and misty morning Dr X takes me to an
adjacent jungle
The writhing snake on his right hand and the leash of
his ferocious leopard in his left hand
Dr X cuddles and smooches them
The sight terrifying

Suddenly, Dr X screeches, looking at me: Run Sandy,
run; they love the morning run
From the corner of my eye I could see Dr X having
unleashed them

74

Instinctively, I run into the thickness of the jungle,
crazy, as if the crucible of living centered on the
muscles and ligaments of my legs
It was as if I could listen to the hissing breath of the
leopard and the crooning bells of the snake on my back

I ran and ran and ran; my lungs pumping to fright and
raw terror
Then the tiny lake cradled inside this ancient jungle
with an abandoned temple of Lord Shiva revealed to
me
I leaped inside the lake, resting on the intertwined
branches, twigs and roots of circumventing large trees
I huffed and huffed breathing smoke into the air
forgetful of my chasers
Believing the periphery of this water body would be
my savior
And then I must have fallen unconscious out of
exhaustion
Because I remember nothing after that – nothing at all

What I remember is waking up inside Dr X's heated
living room and he was serving me steaming tea and
almond cookies and English teacakes and smirked: A
good run, you fatso, Sandy; you should do this every
morning, man, to keep you fit and agile

Moments passed

Dr X looked at me intently sipping his fourth serving of

Americano and told me:

Sandy, life is meaningless and full of futilities; yet the struggle to make life happier for one and all will always make you richly happy; try it

Kolkata
January 21, 2020

<u>For Sam Mendes</u>

Sir Samuel Alexander Mendes, Sam Mendes to us all,
Sam and I lived parallel lives in two separate continents
and are still living now
He lives an extraordinary life and I, of course, live an
ordinary life
Yet, we are pals in some ways
A giant moviemaker of art-house pieces and
entertainers, a theater person, screenwriter and
producer
Has been churning out movies that shook my life –
took my life's breath away – at every critical juncture

1999, the year I was betrayed in love like never before,
came *American Beauty*
That blew to smithereens the American dream
Reminding us once again Camus's prophetic words: It
is in self-death that man makes an independent choice

2008, the year of the mother of all gorges in my life
– a split between my past life and afterlife – came
Revolutionary Road
A blow-by-blow scan of a failing marriage and love of
two persons bitterly caught up in their own choices,
neither willing to let off their guard, for each of them
wants to live a happy life and die a happy death
Marriage and love viewed microcosmically under a
telescope, as if

2012, the year I was healing from my depression,
    came the entertainer with a cynical twist, *Skyfall*
An unpredictable Bond story with poetic stunts (not
forgetting Christopher what he did in *Dark Knight* and
                        Inception)
In the end, Bond takes M to Skyfall, Bond's childhood
home in the Scottish Highlands where with the
gamekeeper Kincade they set up booby traps to fight
                      Silva's men
              A unique revenge story

2019, the year I planned to reengineer my career to
take my writing seriously and professionally, came
                        1917
A war epic: a nine-mile journey on foot through a
            deceitfully ravaged landscape of war
To fulfill a mission to call off an attack doomed to fail
soon after the German retreat to the Hindenburg Line
              during Operation Alberich
A story Sam heard from his paternal grandfather Lance
Corporal Alfred Hubert Mendes who later became a
  Trinidad and Tobago novelist and short story writer
A visual story told with love and planning, the camera
weaves the shots as if the tapestry of the whole film
has been produced in one shot, an illusion that pools
the horror in your nervous system with unmatched
                       efficiency

A moment of brilliant visual moving images: Lance
Corporal William Schofield is running, being chased

down by German soldiers among ruins of Ecoust-Saint-Mein, rifling all around, gunshots one after the other, Schofield runs like a hungry leopard chasing a deer, from a pale night into an ultramarine dawn and then, to his relief, jumps into a river, the fall captured for an instant in slow motion

I will take this series of images to my afterlife

1917 brings to the fore the loneliness of a soldier to fulfil a purpose during war time – a type of implicit courage not explored before

Sam with thanks and warm regards to you

Kolkata
January 22, 2020

My abductors took me blindfolded to a forest with a
heady tropical fragrance
As they opened the black scarf over my eyes, I sighted
a low mountain nearby
Tall trees and the soil covered with marshy large yellow
leaves
Mildly warm, mildly cool – overall pleasant
Strangely, the bearded men who kidnapped me from
a highway tearing me apart from my Volkswagen were
sweating and smoking longish local made cigarettes of
leaves and unfiltered tobacco
Enhancing and tinging the fragrance of the forest

The head of the gang looked at me with embarrassment
and spoke a few lines, that meant
They had kidnapped the wrong guy, which was evident
from the colour of my irises
And now that I had seen them all and their hideout
and trail
They could only return me dead
He stressed; there would be no use pleading or
resisting

This unclean guy also mentioned, death would be
painless with three point-blank shots inside my brain
and darkness and eternal silence thereafter

The absurdity of the situation made me laugh and
forget my life
I was in a rotten, hideous isolation chamber where you

lose count of time and gravity

All of a sudden, a riot of colours appeared on the scene
Birds of various colours and splendour:
Keel-billed-toucan,   bird-of-paradise,   cassowary,
eurylaimidae, hoatzin and wreathed-hornbill

Then, I could hear three shots in the distance
Instantly, I fell asleep feeling a painful lump in my head
I entered inside a dream – a colossal bird zoo, a
paradise for ornithologists
I remembered my life

Kolkata
January 23, 2020

I remember the springtime strikes of my youth
As soon as the strike was announced, I would rummage
the newspapers
To know: who had called the strike, what were the
issues involved, and involuntarily estimating the
chances of it becoming a success
If the estimate was correct, and I supported the issues
I would yet be grief-stricken as I would miss a day out
with Debjani

The successful strikes would be the ones when people
spent holidays at their homes dining and playing
street-cricket
Forlorn streets, closed-down bazaars, soundless
railway tracks
White clouds floating in the sky, a nip in the air, bright
sunshine lighting up a silent city
Some protestors at street corners and faraway
crossroads shouting slogans and raising their voices
for demands

At noon craving to see her face I would start my walk
through the silence of the city on foot – an eight
mile stretch from my home to Debjani's carrying her
favourite book

By the time I reached her home I would be enervated
by the excitement of looking at her face through the

window of her study – for during springtime strikes her
parents forbade her from meeting me on the road and
neither was I allowed to come up

I would whistle lustily till the sound reached her ears
Then she would jump up from wherever she was to
the window
Her sorrowful eyes
Her wide angled grin
Her river of hair
Her frailness
And, her waving of Nathaniel Turn's translated book of
Pablo Neruda's melancholy poems
All of these sights together created a throbbing ache in
my heart – on the verge of explosion

In return, from the road, a street dog and an urchin by
my side, I waved back
Rabi Thakur's slim book: *Chitrangada*, to her trilling
delight

We would go back and forth waving our books till our
hands hurt

We would then depart – me to my home, another
eight mile walk and Debjani to her study to practice
her singing lessons

These faded memories jump to the screen of my mind

whenever a springtime strike is announced nowadays
She and I embrace ourselves and shed tears on our
memories

Kolkata
January 24, 2020

I have a live bomb trapped inside my heart
I tear it away from its bloody wells
And throw the simmering lump at the unassuming
IOCL petrol pump where I live
The bomb explodes igniting the petrol and diesel
subterranean tanks
The fire lurks in the air spreading to everything that is
combustible in and around
The cars, the bikes, the pneumatic air tank, the
buildings
The trees, the shrubberies, the gated complexes
named *Daffodils* and *Chrysanthemums*
The trucks that carry sand and aggregates for criminal
syndicates
The cycles and vans that ferry contract wage labourers
The men and women – multimillionaires and ragged –
passing by – caged within their vehicles – scream for
help – having caught fire
There is smoke everywhere – gray and black
The fire burns hard currency notes and plastic money
– the smell of which I love
Two toddlers in red and white school uniform cry and
screech at the circumventing horror

I withdraw from the sexy sight – it gives me a hard-
on; I smoke my Brazilian cigar; masturbate; gulp my
fourth peg of Vat 69 and stride to my convertible Jeep
and get ready for the chase

Meanwhile, the sound – rattling bells – of fire tankers

can be heard in the distance
Hose pipes hissing water into tireless, unending, skyrocketing flames
Policemen, paramilitary forces and detectives – bunch of pissers and bootlickers of their dirty institutional bosses – gather ominously round the scene

Their only cue: Find the wretched bastard who smells of semen and laughs at this gory scene making circles of smoke from his Brazilian cigar, and they know the numberless visage of my convertible Jeep

My parents used to beat me up when I was a child for I was a serial killer of cats; they put me into a rehabilitation center where I burnt up their store and gassed three rats

Ma and Baba used to cry looking at me, pleading with me to leave my violent ways
I would reply to them: Guys, I love it this way, the suffocation of somebody else's death, blood, twisted veins and arteries, a living being gasping for air, fire and smoke, destruction and death

They disowned me legally and I was on my own, loving it that way for I could work as a stateless mercenary earning gold and diamond and loads of cash in return for death and destruction

The mother of all chases begins and I pump up my

Jeep to a hundred miles per hour
The roads are bad – potholes, bulbous blisters, swelling
speed-breakers – I hate these roads so much that I
will bomb these roads permanently someday

The Jeep rolls and dashes over an embankment into a
pool of swampy mud and behind, there are millions of
decorated riflemen taking a shot at me

I focus on a fatso whom I want to kill for his fat disturbs
my line of vision; I take a shot at him from my pistol

Then the bullets rain from million rifles
Inside my brain
Liver
Spleen
Intestine
Crotch and
My knees

Till such time I am immobile and dead

In my death sleep, I congratulate these murderers for
their upcoming medals and promotions

Kolkata
January 25, 2020

I requested Rahul to participate in the flag hoisting
ceremony on the Republic day

He shot me back a note:
I am stateless, Sandy, you know that
I have no boundaries
I have no Constitution
I bow to no flag
I have no national anthem or song
No alphabet, word or sentence is a rule for me
They can only be songs or signals of freedom for me
Every piece of land is mine
Yet, no piece of land is mine
The air is mine
Yet, no parcel of air is mine
The oceans and seas swell and fall for me
They also swell and fall for billions of people

I have no army, navy or air force
I am forever a migrant, without a family or a community
I have no wealth or home
I have only memories of wonderful landscapes and
also, sufferings of migrants and vagrants like me

When I feel hungry, I beg, I have begged from you
Sandy
When I feel thirsty, I drink from rivers or municipal
taps
When I feel lusty, I beg for sex from sex workers in the

shadowy by-lanes of metropolitan cities and towns;
they understand me better than you, Sandy

I roam around with a surge in my heart
I know not what
It keeps me going around the planet from igloos to
deserts to rocky peaks and white-sand beaches

I roam around with a surge in my heart
I know not what
Sometimes, I cry remembering the wretched aboriginal
gypsies who stole me from an accident site and brought
me up
For my mother and father were dead by the time I saw
the light of this earth

Sandy, you are the only chord that connects me to the
civilization
But do not ask me to bow down to a flag
For I am nothing because I am everything
I am those multi-billion atoms that compose Nigel, the
loneliest bird

There are not many differences between you and me,
Sandy
You have adopted civilization and you fear death
I have adopted nature, adopting death

Kolkata
January 26, 2020

The desert valley of prehistoric ashes covered in layers
of white snow – crooked patches of dried blood here
and there
Surrounded by monumental ash mountains – their
peaks crowned in snow
A strip of asphalt and metal piercing through the
desiccated landscape – walled by columns of ice
An ancient river – frozen – and a wry cutting breeze
A glacier on hold
There is no threat of an avalanche; an overcast cloud
threatening to rain sleets of ice

Faraway there are monasteries and monks

I am on the road on my military bike driving north-
east from south-west
Diagonally cutting across the valley

The loneliness of a looming winter in Ladakh daggers
through your heart

In this part of the world, south of Ladakh where I work,
everything is conspiratorial
That is how existence is: Militancy, terrorism,
counterterrorism, espionages, counterespionages,
killings and kidnappings, belonging to a state and
statelessness

Between this mask and that mask, there are millions
of faces

Between this face and that face, there are millions of
masks
Between this organization and that organization –
stateless or otherwise, there are millions of shadow
organisations intertwined among each other
Are you in the military
Are you in the intelligence
Do you belong to a terrorist camp
Are you working for the militia
Are you on this side of the Line of Control or on that
side
Are you stateless or are you a citizen of any particular
state
Are you a mercenary
Are you in the police
Are you a native or a migrant
Are you a tourist
Are you a hitchhiker
Are you a Muslim or a Hindu or a Buddhist
Are you a kidnapper or the kidnapped
Are you a separatist

No answers, only questions obfuscating my line of
view, as I drive my military bike diagonally cutting
across the valley
With a secret mission trapped inside my brain
A contorted smile forming on my face

Thinking of the ravaged and corrupted crisscrosses in
this part of the world that has happened with time;

there are only shadows and no objects to find anymore

I am not sure who I am: slaving for whom and master
of what art

Kolkata
January 27, 2020

I entered the room after ten years
Sooty, dusty, fungus-laden and a pungent smell of rust
all over and webs of spider on damp walls, in the air

Ma left us in 2009 and this room was locked as if
forever: her bedroom
Her Hawaiian guitar, Pakrashi harmonium, furniture
made out of Kashmiri cedar
Gitabitan, Godrej almirah made of finest steel, oil on
gold-plate-gilded canvasses by Uday da: haphazard
schizophrenic sketches of circles and erratic colours,
Ramakrishna kathamrita

The hazy darkness and the ghostly silence and
everything decaying and crumbling
Suddenly, reminded me of Ma's ferocity, yet her ability
to be a darling of gatherings and parties
Her fluffy colossal, in every attempt, two-egg-omelet
with vegetables and milk with softness breathing
inside, an unparalleled delicacy

Possibly, she would not have left us so early
Had I not mistaken her heart stroke as gastro-intestinal
disorder
And, brought her down the stairs from the first floor of
our house to my car

In life people around you count on you
And, by the time you learn from your actions out of
ignorance, a disaster has rocked your boat

I entered the room after ten years
Guilty and sad for ma

A woman with whom I had detached-years of
togetherness after adolescence
Although I took every advantage of her indulgence
every time, everywhere

Kolkata
January 28, 2020

A journal entry of September 26, 1998, that reads as follows:
A pistol with bullets or a vial of toxin
Would relieve me of my anxieties and restlessness
Not their execution but their presence with me
Would be enough to calm my gyrating soul that I can
leave whenever I want to

A journal entry of January 14, 2005, that reads as follows:
Life is burdensome – family, work and trying to live a
decent life
Sometimes I want to abandon and run away; I lack
the courage
The immediate decision to take my life perplexes me
I lack the courage to jump from a skyscraper; I have
tried it twice

A journal entry of July 29, 2009, that reads as follows:
A therapist suggested that I fall in love
I could not tell her that I have been forever in love with
Debarati, and she is out of bounds in Stockholm
But I also know that if I ever got her I would get bored
with her in three-four years
The way I have got bored with other women, men, and
transvestites
I have tried everything to fight with my anxieties and
restlessness

A journal entry of April 11, 2012, that reads as follows:

*I want to get another job, and take revenge on my
present employer*
Some of them are real uncouth and dirty here
*They are jealous of my innovative intuitions and
entrepreneurial skills*
*They just put me down by hard core politicking,
something they know I will avoid and detest*
*Finally, a top psychiatrist has diagnosed me: morbid
hypochondria, and a beginning of delusional, and
hallucinatory phase that could become full-fledged
schizophrenia*

A journal entry of December 12, 2015, that reads as
follows:
I do not go anywhere nowadays
*I do not sleep; it is not required anymore; my body no
longer needs any rest*
*My children did well in their lives; they are somewhere;
I do not remember where*
*My wife takes care of me; she sleeps with Dipanjan in
our bedroom*
*Dipanjan is a pharmaceutical retailer, my school time
friend, a well of cash*
He takes care of financial matters of our household
*Dipanjan and my wife look very beautiful in each
other's arms*
*I sit in my wrought-iron chair in our rotting, and mossy
garden*
*I look at the yellowed photographs of Ma, Baba, and
Tinni, in snow at Kulu, my little sister*

They all left me very early in life; I don't know why
The sky is a relief to look at
The sky is a relief to look at
The sky is a relief to look at

Bhopal
January 29, 2020

You have been such a debauch all your life, although
you have been close to a genius
Ma has been an equal debauch, an intellectual socialite
You both shattered my childhood with no attachment
to trust human relationships
Although, you both loved me, pampered me, and
indulged me in your own ways
But, I was always fearful and nervous, that you would
act repeatedly out of unfaithfulness to each other
And, then you had bitter quarrels, and abused each
other, hurling profanities
An aggressively raucous houseboat
That caged a child with perpetual fear, and palpitation
that the houseboat might explode all of a sudden
leaving all the three faraway from each other, and the
child homeless

Rony thundered Rahul on a long-distance call

Rahul did not reply, he cried silently so that Rony could
not hear

Baba, are you there?
I have trust issues in my own relationships now
And, that drives me mad
Takes away the beauty of companionship
Maybe I will be robbed of genuine love in my life for
the ghosts you have planted in my soul in my unhappy
childhood

Yet, I want to discuss my trust issues with you, because
in you I find an unwavering anchor borne out of our
later years together

Now I understand: debauchery is a result of the way
you are built, a part of it can be controlled, and a part
of it you have to give in to

Baba, I want a family of devoted man and wife with
angel-like children hopping around us

Baba, help me build trust in the woman I love, for you
have witnessed the extremities of life

Rahul cries at the other end of the telephone line;
imploring to himself

The world has changed so much in the intervening
years
The world has changed so much in the intervening
years
The world has changed so much in the intervening
years

Devoted love as a phenomenon is a dying art

Rahul knew he would stand by his son
Not sure, whether he was the right man to stand by
his son

The telephone line clicked and dropped dead

Kolkata
January 30, 2020

You took me to your land full of
Trees of royal poinciana, African tulip, trumpet, cassia,
gold medallion, coral, silk floss, golden pendas, orchid
and jacaranda
You undressed me and made love to me like the queen
of your forest
Then we fell asleep in each other's arms, naked on a
bed of leaves and flowers on tropical soil, the scents of
our bodies soaring up in the sky

We dreamed of our tree-house on a banyan fig with
massive trunk and aerial roots for support

We have lived inside the crucible of civilization for so
long that we grew tired of it
Always planning to run away to distant lands, be on
oceans and be on the road

Our friends would say: Because you do not have
children and you have substantial inheritance, you can
afford to lead a life of explorers

This was not untrue but nobody appreciated our
wanderlust, our ability to move beyond stativity and
accumulation of wealth for oneself

Lily and I cared less of what others said although we
loved their company otherwise for people are like trees
of differing species, they are interesting and good to
know

The building up of our tree-house was a test in hard
work, skill and patience

The housewarming ceremony was a silent affair amidst
the unique sound of the forest

And, then Lily and I made love in slow motion through
the moon lit night among strange calls of birds and
animals inside the forest

Kolkata
January 31, 2020